HARRY LEARNS
FRENCH

Illustrated by Annabel Tempest
Written by Sue Finnie & Danièle Bourdais

ticktock
MEDIA

Copyright © *ticktock* Entertainment Ltd. 2002
Unit 2, Orchard Business Centre, North Farm Road, Tunbridge Wells, TN2 3XF.
First published in Great Britain in 2002 by *ticktock* Media Ltd.,
Text by Sue Finnie and Danièle Bourdais
Illustrations by Annabel Tempest
ISBN 1 86007 301 8
Printed in Hong Kong.
A CIP catalogue record for this book is available from the British Library.

Bonjour!

Welcome to France. This book is your ticket on a whistle-stop tour of this beautiful country, and a great introduction to the French language.

1 Read

Follow Harry and Léa's adventures in France as they go to the beach, visit a farm and much more.

2 Learn

All the French words in this book are in **bold.** If you want to find out what they mean, turn to the handy phrasebook on each page. To help you speak French, there is also an easy-to-follow guide to pronunciation.

3 Listen

The CD-Rom completes the experience. Each screen you see is identical to the pages in the book, so you can hear the spoken French. There are games too, to help you along. Load up the disk and get clicking!

- **SORTIE** ▸▸
- **ARRIVÉES** ▴
- **RENSEIGNEMENTS** ◂◂
- **DÉPARTS** ◂◂
- **TRAINS** ▸▸
- **AUTOBUS** ▸▸
- **TAXIS** ▸▸
- **TOILETTES** ▾▾

Harry can't believe he's already in France! He loved being in the plane, on top of the clouds. Now he is going to meet Léa Bertin and her family. He'll be staying with them for a week.

How would you say your name in French?

Je m'appelle...

What will he say? It's lucky he has a little phrasebook. It will come in handy. (It will help you too!)

"**Bonjour, Harry!**" says a voice near him. It must be Léa saying hello!
"**Je m'appelle Léa!**" says the girl. Yes, it is Léa. "**Bonjour!**" says Harry
excitedly as he is introduced to her family.

C'est mon papa.

C'est ma maman.

C'est ma sœur, Zoé.

C'est mon frère, Louis.

C'est ma sœur, Chloé.

SORTIE

Harry's Phrasebook

"C'est la maison!" says Monsieur Bertin, pointing at the house. Léa can't wait to show Harry her pets. There is Minou the cat, Jeannot the pet rabbit, and Filou the dog. But Filou is nowhere to be seen. **"Où est Filou?"** asks Léa.

Harry's
Phrasebook

rue de
quimper

Can you
find Filou?

Filou
est dans...

la salle de bains

le lavabo

la baignoire

les toilettes

la chambre

l'armoire

le lit

la cuisine

la cuisinière

la table

la chaise

Le chat est dans la cuisine.

le salon

le canapé

la télé

le fauteuil

Le lapin est dans le salon.

It's lunchtime. At first, Harry doesn't feel very hungry.
"Tu veux des carottes?" asks Madame Bertin.
He's not sure he wants any carrots, he doesn't have them like that at home. Just a bit to try then... Mmm, yummy!

Je voudrais des carottes, s'il vous plaît.

des carottes

de l'eau

de la salade

du pain

du gâteau au chocolat

du poulet

des fruits

des haricots verts

du fromage

Look at the table and say what you would like for lunch.

Je voudrais...

He'd like more carrots, and chicken, and green beans too, and salad, and cheese, and bread...

... and lots of chocolate cake! Harry really, really loves chocolate!
"C'est bon?" asks Madame Bertin. Oh, yes, it's nice, very nice!
"C'est très bon!" says Harry, with a
chocolate-covered smile on his
chocolate-covered face!

Mmm, c'est bon!

Harry's
Phrasebook

Harry's Phrasebook

Next day it is warm and sunny, perfect for going to the beach. **"On joue?"** asks Léa. Good idea, let's play! Harry can't wait to show off his football skills to his new friend! **"Tu aimes bien le foot?"** he asks. **"Non"** replies Léa.

le foot

le badminton

le frisbee

le château de sable

Harry can't believe it: Léa doesn't like football! **"Tu aimes bien les boules?"** asks Léa. **"Oui, j'aime bien les boules,"** Harry says nodding, although he's not quite sure how to play!

la planche à voile

la nage

les boules

la pêche

la balle

Look at the beach and say what you like doing.

J'aime bien...

Léa shows Harry how to play boules: first you throw the little ball and then you throw the bigger ones as close to it as possible. The person who throws the nearest ball wins a point. Harry plays with the red and blue balls. Léa plays with the yellow and green balls. Who wins the point?

What is your favourite colour?

Ma couleur préférée, c'est...

Oh no! Harry's boule has landed in the ice cream! The man looks really cross. Harry's very sorry. **"Pardon, monsieur!"**, he apologises. If only Léa would come and help him out!

But Léa is too busy laughing!

Harry's Phrasebook

Harry's
Phrasebook

un cheval

un canard

une chèvre

une poule

The next day, Harry and Léa go to the farm belonging to Léa's grandpa. Harry is very excited. **"Tu aimes les animaux?,"** asks Léa. Harry loves animals, and can't wait to explore **Grand-père** Bertin's farm.

un taureau

un mouton

un cochon

une vache

What animals can you see?

Il y a...

Harry goes exploring. There are hens everywhere, and plenty of eggs to collect!
Harry wonders how many he'll find: **"Un, deux, trois, quatre, cinq, six,
sept, huit, neuf, dix!"** Ten eggs!

Grand-père takes Léa to see some cute little piglets, just two days old. Léa picks one up. *"Il est petit!"* Yes, it is tiny. But not all farm animals are tiny and cute. Harry is looking at the bull. *"Il est gros!"* he laughs.

How many piglets can you count?

Un, deux...

The bull is big, VERY big and he looks cross, VERY cross! Run, Filou!

Saturday the 14th of July is a special day in France. It is the French National Day. To celebrate, Madame Bertin is organising a picnic for the children. She asks Harry and Léa to do some shopping in the village. **"N'oubliez pas le pain!"** she repeats. They must not forget the bread, it is very important.

la boucherie

la maison de la presse

LA POISSONNERIE

la charcuterie

le vélo

la voiture

Harry's Phrasebook

Harry looks at all the shops along the main street. They look a bit different from those at home and he'd love to have a look in all of them.

Which shop would sell fish? A magazine? Some apples?

le magasin de jouets

le supermarché

la boulangerie

le bus

Harry can't believe his eyes when he sees all the lovely things in the **boulangerie**, especially the chocolate cakes. Léa buys lots of treats for the picnic.

When their basket is full, Léa and Harry head home. Madame Bertin will be very pleased with them. Or will she? Haven't they forgotten something, one very important thing?

Oui, mademoiselle.

une baguette

un pain

une tarte

un pain au chocolat

un croissant

un éclair

which of these things would you like?

Je voudrais...

After going back to get the bread from the **boulangerie,** they pop into the **magasin de jouet.** Harry loves toys shops, and would just love to get that brilliant football in the window. But first, he wants to buy presents for all his family and friends.

le ballon

la carte postale

le t-shirt

la casquette

le stylo

le porte-clef

le pin's

le jeu

le livre

le poster

Harry finds lots of lovely things for everyone. As he's got a bit of money left, he wants to know how much the football is. **"C'est combien, le ballon?"** he asks. It costs six euros. **"Un, deux, trois, quatre..."** Oh no, he hasn't got enough! He is almost tempted to give back the present for his sister!

Harry's Phrasebook

Choose a
costume
for a fancy
dress party!

Je suis...

The rest of the way home, Harry can't stop thinking about the football. Then, just in front of Léa's house, they see a group of Léa's friends, all out in fancy dress. **"Je suis un fantôme!"** says a familiar voice.

une fée

un pirate

un fantôme

un gendarme

un astronaute

une infirmière

un cowboy

Harry remembers that the picnic today is a fancy dress picnic!

Harry and Léa run in to choose their costumes. Harry looks at all the clothes on the bed. What are Harry and Léa going to be?

une robe

ne veste

un haut

un chapeau

une jupe

des bottes

un pantalon

Harry's Phrasebook

un short

des chaussures

As Harry the footballer and Princess Léa tuck into the delicious food at the picnic, Harry realises that he is going home tomorrow. The week in France has gone by in a flash. The beach, the farm, the picnic...

un pique-nique

une princesse

un footballeur

His Mum and Dad won't believe how many French words he has learnt!

At the airport, Harry gives Monsieur and Madame Bertin a kiss on each cheek and thanks them: **"Au revoir, monsieur, au revoir, madame... merci!"** Léa has a surprise for Harry. It's the football, the one Harry wanted so much! **"Oh merci, Léa, merci!"** beams Harry.

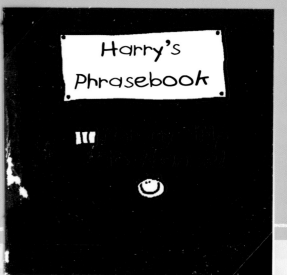

Harry's Phrasebook

Harry would love to come back to France next year, to see Léa and her family. In his loudest voice, he calls out with a last wave: **"À bientôt!"** See you again soon!

My French Holiday Scrapbook

Léa's village

French money is called the Euro.

The French flag is called the Tricolore.

French stamps